MW01252021

Servants of the Lord

STUDY GUIDE and LEADERS NOTES

Marian Baden, Joan Gerber, Carolyn Sims

LWML Consultant: Carol Zehnder

Edited by Thomas J. Doyle

CONCORDIA PUBLISHING HOUSE · SAINT LOUIS

Acknowledgment

The International Lutheran Women's Missionary League Christian Growth Committee has consulted with the editor and authors in the development of this Bible study, and recommends its use.

Assistant to the Editor: Cindi Crismon

Scripture quotations are taken from THE HOLY BIBLE, NEW INTERNATIONAL VERSION®. Copyright © 1973, 1978, 1984 by the International Bible Society. Used by permission of Zondervan Publishing House. All rights reserved.

The "NIV" and "New International Version" trademarks are registered in the United States Patent and Trademark Office by the International Bible Society. Use of either trademark requires the permission of the International Bible Society.

7 8 9 10 11 12 13   08 07 06 05 04 03 02

Contents

Study Guide

Leaders Notes

Introduction

Welcome to a fresh, new look at servanthood. Although the stories of the women in this study may be familiar to you, you are about to be challenged to look deeper than you ever have.

Within the framework of the opening and closing worship, there will be a trip into the past (her story), a trip into the present (your story), and a trip into the future (what's next?). You will be offered personal projects that will make each servant's story a reality for you. For example, Hannah's Old Testament song will be compared to Mary's New Testament Magnificat, and you will get to compare both of them with your own song. All of this is combined with lively humor that helps you to realize the bond you have with each sister in Christ who lived so long ago.

As you study the six servants, see Christ in their lives. See Christ in your life. See that His great example of leadership is ...
SERVANTHOOD.

Christian Growth Committee
International Lutheran Women's Missionary League

Miriam

First String or Second Fiddle?

Theme

God calls and equips His people for service. Sin, however, taints our motives and prevents us from doing God's will. Just as God refocused Miriam's attention from herself to Himself, called her to repentance, and graphically healed her both physically and spiritually so He also calls, directs, and heals us through faith in Jesus Christ. By the power of the Holy Spirit working through us, we, too, are able to serve in God-pleasing ways.

Objectives

That by the power of the Spirit working through God's Word, we will

1. identify the motives for our service and the gifts that God has given us;
2. repent of our self-centered goals and receive Christ's forgiveness for them;
3. adopt an attitude of giving that focuses on God's direction and the needs of those whom we serve rather than on any glory we might receive;
4. serve gladly and without reservation those whom God entrusts to our care.

Opening Worship

Leader: Almighty God, Father, Son, and Holy Spirit, we celebrate Your presence because You have promised that wherever two or more are gathered in Your name, You are among us.

Participants: We are here, Lord, to learn of Your ways and to be empowered by the Holy Spirit working through Your Word.

Leader: Open our ears

Participants: And tell us of Your saving grace in Christ Jesus.

Leader: Open our eyes

Participants: And show us Your example for our lives.

Leader: Open our minds

Participants: And explain Your will.

Leader: Open our arms

Participants: And enable us to do Your work.

Leader: Open our hearts

Participants: And move us to love You and all Your people because You first loved us.

Leader: For Jesus' sake,

All: Amen.

Into the Lesson

Read Exodus 15:19–21.

Which of the following well-known persons would best depict Miriam's character in the movie version of her life? Why?

Audrey Hepburn
Mother Teresa
Bette Midler
Other _____

How would she be billed? Why?

A supporting role
Late in the credits
A STAR!
Other _____

Miriam was a tambourine kind of person. If there was singing, she would lead it. If there was dancing, she would teach the steps. Choosing instruments? Make hers percussion, and make it loud. By the way, Miriam was over 90 years old when this event occurred!

There was no question as to who was directing the choir. In front of everybody, leading the way was Miriam. She loved it. She was good at it. She joyfully served God through her leadership.

Do you know someone like her? Are *you* someone like her? Do you usually find yourself in a leading role, eager to take charge? Is it possible to lead and serve at the same time, or are the two contradictory? The answer to that question lies in your response when somebody else comes along with a bigger tambourine. What happens when you do the work, and someone else gets the credit? Watch what happened to Miriam.

Into the Past

1. Read Exodus 2:1–10 and Exodus 15:20–21. On the basis of these verses, what qualities did Miriam possess that made her a good leader? The name Miriam means "rebelliously." Is rebelliousness a necessary component of leadership? Why?

2. How was Miriam able to use these qualities in leadership roles?

3. Exodus 15:24 refers to Miriam as prophetess. Who are some other prophetesses mentioned in Scripture?

   Judges 4:4
   2 Kings 22:14
   Luke 2:36
   Acts 21:8–9

   What did they all have in common?

4. What was Miriam's relationship to Moses and Aaron (Numbers 26:59)? What role do you suppose Miriam had in her family as she was growing up?

5. Miriam was busy doing the Lord's work. She was respected among her family and peers. She had experienced firsthand God's miracles of deliverance. What more could she possibly want? Read Numbers 12:1–15.

6. What excuse did Miriam and Aaron give for their dissatisfaction with Moses?

Moses' wife was a descendant of Cush. Cush was the first son of Ham, the ancestor of people living in the southern Nile Valley. For Moses to marry a Gentile was, indeed, not in line with God's will. But the issue here was not Moses' relationship with his wife. The issue was Moses' relationship with God. Can't you just hear Miriam whine to Aaron?

"God always liked Moses best. He thinks he is so perfect. Doesn't He know Moses married a *Cushite*? Why does Moses get all the credit? We've prophesied, too. We have musical and artistic talents, besides. Nobody appreciates all the work we do. I've played the tambourine until my ears rattled, and I've danced until the burning sand blistered my feet (all out of love for the Lord, of course). Why does Moses get all the glory? What's wrong with God, anyway?"

Miriam had gone too far.

7. Describe God's response to Miriam's outburst.

8. True, Miriam deserved a reprimand. But, leprosy? Miriam's well-planned life of leadership was destroyed. You don't feel like singing when you have leprosy. You can't play the tambourine with deformed hands. No one comes close enough to

hear you prophesy. Even Moses was struck with horror when he considered her fate. What was Moses' reaction (Numbers 12:13)?

9. Why do you think God was so harsh with Miriam?

The God whose deliverance from Pharaoh Miriam had once celebrated was still in the deliverance business. After seven days (a symbol of completion), He delivered her again and restored Miriam to her position of service.

What did the people do while Miriam was confined outside camp? They didn't journey on without her. They valued her enough to wait. Her years of service among them had meant something after all—not because her service was so great, but because the God she served was so great.

10. The Bible records no more of Miriam's songs. If she had sung on the day her leprosy was healed, what might she have said?

Into the Present

List some talents or gifts God has given you.

List some ways you currently serve God in your family, community, or church.

Which of the following famous people could best play the role of your life in a movie?

Meryl Streep

Mother Teresa

Bette Midler

Other _____

What is your instrument?

Tambourine

Flute

First Violin

Second Fiddle

Other _____

Can you think of a time you went to a great deal of work and someone else got the credit for it? How did you feel? What did you do?

Jesus provides complete forgiveness from our sinful attitudes and motives. His love for us motivates us to imitate His attitude and actions of service. Read Philippians 2:5–11. How did Jesus' attitude differ from Miriam's? Although He was fully God, He willingly did not fully use His power, but was content to play "second fiddle." What was His ultimate act of service? What was its result? How does His service to us affect our service to Him and others?

Rank the following opportunities for service from easy to very difficult on a five-point scale (0 = easy; 5 = very difficult):

_____ Staying home from work with a sick infant.

_____ Taking care of an elderly neighbor while his wife is shopping.

_____ Teaching a Sunday school class.

_____ Singing in the choir.

_____ Singing a solo.

_____ Giving a homeless person a room in your house.

_____ Visiting a sick friend in the hospital.

_____ Calling on visitors to the church.

_____ Praying for a convicted child molester.

_____ Cleaning house for a disabled person.

_____ Forgiving a family member or friend who has caused you grief.

_____ Complimenting a person who is boastful of his or her accomplishments.

What makes some of these acts easy?

What makes some of these acts difficult?

Whom are you serving in each one?

How does knowing that your service is really to the Lord make even the most unglamorous and unrewarded task possible?

Our redemption through Jesus Christ, our Deliverer, compels and empowers us to serve. It makes no difference if we are recognized or given credit by other people. God knows what He has done for us. He knows how we react in gratitude to Him. He declares all our service to be "first string" regardless of its apparent success or failure because He sees it as perfect, He counts Jesus' life of complete and perfect service to be ours.

Knowing that our efforts are already successful in God's eyes frees us to give without fear of failure or rejection. When God hands us the tambourine, or flute, or fiddle, He wants us to play it for all we are worth, for the music is His, and so are we!

Regarding Your Church Family

Pray together the Lord's Prayer. Emphasize the words *Thy* and *Thine* each time they are spoken. Focusing on our heavenly Father draws the attention away from ourselves. When His will is done we can be sure that, whether we lead or follow, we are truly serving Him.

Into the Future

Try doing one of the activities you ranked as "easy" or "difficult" this week. How far up the "difficult" scale can you reach?

Pray for someone who is in a position of leadership in your church.

Do an act of service anonymously. Let it be a secret between God and you.

Read Exodus 15:21 and complete the last portion with an act of deliverance God has worked in your life:

"Sing to the Lord, for He is highly exalted. He has . . . "

Closing Worship

Sing or read together the hymn "Lord of Glory, You Have Bought Us."

> Lord of glory, You have bought us
> With Your lifeblood as the price,
> Never grudging for the lost ones
> That tremendous sacrifice;
> And with that have freely given
> Blessings countless as the sand
> To th'unthankful and the evil
> With Your own unsparing hand.
>
> Grant us hearts, dear Lord, to give You
> Gladly, freely of Your own.
> With the sunshine of Your goodness
> Melt our thankless hearts of stone
> Till our cold and selfish natures,
> Warmed by You, at length believe
> That more happy and more blessed
> 'Tis to give than to receive.
>
> Wondrous honor You have given
> To our humblest charity
> In Your own mysterious sentence,
> "You have done it all to Me."

Can it be, O gracious Master,
　　That You deign for alms to sue,
Saying by Your poor and needy,
　　"Give as I have giv'n to you"?

Yes, the sorrow and the suff'rings
　　Which on ev'ry hand we view
Channels are for gifts and off'rings
　　Due by solemn right to You;
Right of which we may not rob You,
　　Debt we may not chose but pay
Lest that face of love and pity
　　Turn from us another day.

Lord of glory, You have bought us
　　With Your lifeblood as the price,
Never grudging for the lost ones
　　That tremendous sacrifice.
Give us faith to trust You boldly,
　　Hope, to stay our souls on You;
But, oh, best of all Your graces,
　　With Your love our love renew. Amen.

Deborah

"I Will Go with You"

Theme

The people of Israel were in trouble once again because they did evil in the sight of the Lord. And once again, God provided them with a rescuer. Just as He provided not only a rescuer and victory for the Israelites through the person and work of Deborah, so He also provides us with a rescuer and victory through the person and work of Jesus Christ. The best news of all is that God has already given us victory over sin, death, and the power of Satan. His love for us empowers us to serve Him as both leader and supporter.

Objectives

That by the power of the Holy Spirit working through God's Word, we will

1. demonstrate the courage to step out in faith, to do what needs to be done in order to serve the Lord;
2. articulate the confidence that the Lord will go with us, whatever our task;
3. recognize that God provided a rescuer, Jesus, who willingly suffered and died on the cross to win for us full and complete forgiveness for our sins.

Opening Worship

Speak the litany together.

Leader: When we are afraid of the unknown,
All: "I will go with you," says the Lord.
Leader: When we need to confront a friend or family member,
All: "I will go with you," says the Lord.
Leader: When we need to speak out in our church or in the
community,
All: "I will go with you," says the Lord.
Leader: When we need to change our own behavior,
All: "I will go with you," says the Lord.

Sing or speak together the first stanza of "God of Grace and God of Glory."

God of grace and God of glory,
On Your people pour Your pow'r;
Crown Your ancient church's story;
Bring its bud to glorious flow'r.
Grant us wisdom, grant us courage
For the facing of this hour,
For the facing of this hour.

Into the Lesson

Foot-dragging is a problem among Christians. Often we know what the Lord would have us do, but we don't want to do it, so we drag our feet. Trace around your foot. On it write three challenges, areas in which you could step out in faith, things you believe the Lord wants you to do that you have delayed.

Into the Past

The story of Deborah is a chronicle of two women of courage—Deborah and Jael—and how the Lord used them to accomplish His purpose. Look up the following Bible verses and match them to these possible headlines from newspapers at the time of Deborah's rule.

Judges	Headlines
4:1–3	1. _____ Sisera's Troops Annihilated
4:3	2. _____ Sisera Killed as He Seeks Refuge
	3. _____ Israelites Chafe under Jabin's Rule
4:4–5	4. _____ Sisera's Mother Awaits His Return
4:6a	5. _____ Israelites Plead for Relief
4:6b	6. _____ Barak Summoned to Deborah's Palm
4:7	7. _____ Sisera Flees to Kenite Clan
4:8	8. _____ 10,000 Men of Naphtali and Zebulun Drafted by God
4:12–13	9. _____ Deborah Serves as Judge to Replace Shamgar
4:15	10. _____ 900 Chariots Abandoned
4:16	11. _____ Israel Enters 40 Years of Peace
4:17	12. _____ God Lures Sisera's Army to Kishon River
4:17–22	13. _____ Commander of Army Refuses to Go into Battle without the Support of a Woman
5:28	
5:31	14. _____ Sisera's Forces Armed and Ready

Into the Present

Vaya con Dios—Go with God

1. What excuses might Deborah have given for not going along with Barak and his army?

2. The imperative *go* was a common command of God to His people. "Oh no, I won't go," was and is an all too common response. In Deborah's case, it was Barak saying "I'll go if you'll go." Sometimes today we say, "You go first."
   Look up the following passages about other reluctant goers.

   Jonah 1:1–2
   God directed _____ to _____.
   Judges 6:14–16
   God directed _____ to _____.
   Exodus 3:10
   God directed _____ to _____.

   In each case God empowered His servants to obey. Through faith God enabled those who were once reluctant, or at times downright obstinate, to accomplish great things for Him.

3. Now read Matthew 28:19–20. What is God's imperative to us today?

4. What are some of the excuses we sometimes give for not stepping out in faithful service today?

5. What motivates us to respond to God's command "Go!" by going? See Ephesians 2:4–10 for the reason for joyfully stepping out in service to Him.

6. Deborah's gifts seem to have included discernment, common sense, intuition, fairness, and conflict resolution skills.

   Trace around your hand. On each finger, write one characteristic with which God has gifted you and tell how you could use it in service to Him.

Regarding Your Church Family

God chose and empowered Deborah to lead and support General Barak.

1. What opportunities has God provided you to either lead and/or support in your congregation?

2. How might you be a leader as you support others—male or female—who are in leadership in your congregation?

3. Share some times or instances in which God has enabled you to step out in service to Him as either a leader or a supporter of leadership.

4. How can serving God as a supporter sometimes be more difficult then serving Him as a leader?

Into the Future

1. Deborah said to Barak, "I will go with you." Think of someone who needs your support. Write a letter of encouragement to that person or plan to go with the person while he or she tackles a difficult task. Tell or remind the person that not only you but the Lord will go with him or her.

2. Deborah was in a position of authority in her community. What change would you promote if you had such authority (such as a supreme court justice of the United States)?

3. Chapter five of Judges is a song of victory addressed to God. Many scholars consider Deborah's song to be one of the earliest existing examples of Hebrew poetry. It gives God the glory and shows a living faith in a time of national disunity.

   Many women have written religious poetry in the form of hymns. Sing together some of these well-known hymns written by women.

The following hymns were written by Frances R. Havergal:

"O Savior, Precious Savior"
"Take My Life, O Lord, Renew"
"I Am Trusting You, Lord Jesus"
"Now the Light Has Gone Away"

Other women wrote the following hymns:

"Drawn to the Cross, Which You Have Blessed," by
Genevieve Irons
"At the Name of Jesus," by Caroline M. Noel
"Lord, Take My Hand and Lead Me," by Julie von Hausmann
"Be Still, My Soul," by Catharina von Schlegel
"Hosanna, Loud Hosanna," by Jeanette Threlfall
"Nearer, My God, to Thee," by Sarah F. Adams
"Lord of Glory, You Have Bought Us," by Eliza S. Alderson
"Speak, O Lord, Your Servant Listens," by Anna Sophia of
Hesse-Darmstadt
"Lord, to You Immortal Praise," by Anna Barbauld
"We Praise You, O God," by Julia C. Cory
"Just as I Am, Without One Plea," by Charlotte Elliott
"O Perfect Love," by Dorothy F. Gurney

4. What are some examples of specific instances in which God rescued you? Think about a time when God strengthened you beyond your means. Write a song-poem about it.

Closing Worship

Sing or speak the words of one or more of the hymns written by women.

Pray, "Lord God, You have called Your servants to ventures of which we cannot see the ending, by paths as yet untrodden, through perils unknown. Give us faith to go out with good courage, not knowing where we go, but only that Your hand is leading us and Your love supporting us; through Jesus Christ, our Lord. Amen."

Hannah

Return to Sender

Theme

Hannah realized that only God could fulfill her desperate desire to have a child. In His good time God answered Hannah's prayer. Hannah responded to God's gracious gift by giving her son and his life in service to the Lord. God supplies us, too, with spiritual and physical resources according to His good will and purely out of His mercy and grace. We are totally dependent upon Him for all blessings, including the gift of faith in Jesus, through which He grants us eternal life with Him in heaven. As He supplies us all that we need to support our physical and spiritual lives, we are motivated and empowered to give our time, talents, and treasures in service to Him and others.

Objectives

That by the power of the Holy Spirit working through God's Word, we will

1. recognize Hannah's longing for a child and her feelings of inadequacy as a barren woman in the society of her day;
2. realize, as Hannah did, our dependence on God for all physical and spiritual blessings;
3. thank God for His blessings, especially His gift of salvation through Jesus Christ;
4. live lives of blessing to others, giving in return the time, talents, and treasures that God has given to us.

25

Opening Worship

Leader: For all the blessings You have given us, merciful Father,
Participants: We thank You.
Leader: For our homes and daily provisions,
Participants: We thank You.
Leader: For families and people who love us,
Participants: We thank You.
Leader: For Jesus, our Savior, and His death for us on the cross,
Participants: We praise You.
Leader: For being impatient when Your timing is different from ours,
Participants: Forgive us for Jesus' sake.
Leader: Since You have given us everything,
Participants: Accept our praise.
Leader: Since You have given us everything,
Participants: Accept our service.
Leader: Since You have given us everything,
Participants: Accept our lives, for we belong to You. Amen.

Into the Lesson

Dear Sadie,

I have never written a letter to you before, but my life is becoming intolerable. My husband loves his other wife better than me. I have done everything I can to win his favor. I have borne him children, which she has not. Still he insists on giving her whatever she wants. I've even tried making her life so miserable she will leave us all in peace, but she continues to whine and sulk and demand his attention. What shall I do? (Please do not use my real name. This is a small town.)

Signed,
Loving, but Unloved (Peninnah)

Dear Sadie,

I have never written a letter to you before, but my life is miserable. I want to have a baby—a son to carry on my husband's name and grow up to honor God, but I just can't get pregnant. My husband says he loves me anyway; yet in his eyes I see the pain. To make matters worse, he has taken another wife who taunts and ridicules me because she has many children and I have none. Her cutting remarks really hurt. I can't stand her hatefulness much longer. I pray, but God doesn't seem to be listening. What shall I do? (Please do not use my real name; this is a small town.)

Signed,
Loved, but Loveless (Hannah)

Dear Sadie,

Help! I am married to two women who are constantly fighting with each other. My first wife was barren so I married another in order to have children to carry on my name. It seemed like a good idea at the time, but what a mistake! I really love my first wife best. Why can't she focus her attention on me instead of complaining? I don't need her for children; I love her for herself. My second wife won't let the other one alone. Her jealousy is driving me crazy. What shall I do? (Please don't use my real name; this is a small town.)

Signed,
Just Wants Peace (Elkanah)

There seems to be major turmoil in the Elkanah household. Two wives, a frustrating situation, and no solution in sight make for big trouble. Before "Dear Sadie" pens her reply, let's take a look at what prompted the letters.

Into the Past

Read 1 Samuel 1:1–2:11.

1. Fill in the blanks according to the facts of the story.

Fact/Event	Consequence/Result	Feeling
Hannah was barren (1:1–2)		
Elkanah loved Hannah more (1:3–6)		
Hannah was distraught (1:6–11)		
Eli sees Hannah (1:12–14)		
Hannah explains (1:15–18)		
Hannah has a child (1:19–20)		
Hannah keeps her vow (1:21–28)		

2. Put a + in the margin at the point at which Hannah's feelings changed from despair to joy. What caused this transformation?

3. To Hannah the frustration of infertility was amplified beyond normal maternal yearnings. Why was it so important for Hebrew women to bear children? Search the following verses for the answer:

Genesis 1:28

Deuteronomy 28:4

Luke 1:25

2 Kings 4:11–14

4. Hannah felt more like a withered weed than the fruitful vine she longed to be. What was it that bothered her most about being barren? What did she want to give that a childless woman could not?

5. Year after year Hannah and Elkanah came to the house of the Lord, faithful to His command. What feast were they celebrating (Exodus 23:14–17; Leviticus 23:39–43)?

6. To what modern-day harvest celebration might this feast be compared? How might the focus of this event have added to Hannah's feelings of depression?

7. Once more, as she had doubtless done many times before, Hannah poured out her prayer to the Lord. How did she address Him in 1 Samuel 1:11?

8. In other words, Hannah addressed God as the sovereign over all powers in heaven and earth. "Surely," she was declaring, "the God who can control all the powers of the universe can create one little baby in my otherwise worthless womb."

Then, with tears streaming down her face, she went one step further.

What did she promise (1 Samuel 1:11)?

9. Was Hannah actually trying to bargain with God? Was she striking a deal to manipulate Him into giving in to her wishes?

10. Hannah's tears of sadness soon turned to tears of joy. God gave, as she knew He would, the child for which she had prayed. Verse 19 says that God "remembered" her. Had He really forgotten?

11. List some benefits Hannah received through her years of waiting.

12. Hannah's song in 1 Samuel 2:1–10 has been called the Magnificat of the Old Testament. Compare it with Mary's song of praise in Luke 1:46–55.

Into the Present

1. If you were "Dear Sadie," how would you reply to the three letters you received?

2. Prayer is the response of God's people to the love and forgiveness He provides to them through faith in Christ Jesus. List below things for which you have prayed that fall into the following categories:

Prayers Answered Immediately	Prayers Answered after Waiting	Prayers Not Answered Yet

How is God's loving care for you evident in each of His responses?

3. Suppose God had chosen to answer Hannah's prayer by not giving her a child. Suppose it was His will to give her other avenues of service. Would the tone of her song in 1 Samuel 2:1–2 still be the same? What/Who was the object of her praise—the gift or the giver?

4. What was God's ultimate gift to us (John 3:16)?

Fertile or childless, rich or unqualified for credit, healthy or disabled, optimistic or depressed, in all conditions we are by God's grace through faith in Jesus God's redeemed people. Like Hannah, through the power of the Holy Spirit, our hearts trust the God whose wisdom surpasses our own, whose love is unfailing, and whose power controls the universe. When He answers our prayers, in His own time and way, we will praise Him, returning to Him what He chooses to give. Then our lives and all we possess are truly dedicated to His service. His generosity exceeds our wildest dreams.

Regarding Your Church Family

Imagine how different life could have been for Hannah if Peninnah had prayed with her. Think of people in your church who have needs and desires that are unfulfilled. Do you know a family with a disabled or rebellious child? Is a father out of work? Does your pastor seem tired and discouraged? Pray for them this week assured that God will answer your prayers.

Into the Future

1. If you have children or grandchildren encourage them to consider dedicating themselves to the Lord's service as a full-time worker in the church. Write to one of our synodical colleges or universities for information. Pray that your children/grandchildren will seek and know God's will for their lives. If you have no children of your own, identify a young person in your congregation who you think would make a good church worker. Encourage him or her with your interest, discussion, and prayers.

2. Pray that God would continue to provide you many opportunities to serve Him with the time, talents, and treasures He has given to you.

Closing Worship

Write a prayer request on a slip of paper, put it into a box, and draw out of the box a prayer request written by someone else. Incorporate these petitions into a circle prayer. You may take turns praying aloud or you may pray silently. Take the prayer slip home with you to pray about during the week.

Sing or pray together the hymn "We Give You But Your Own."

> We give You but Your own
> In any gifts we bring;
> All that we have is Yours alone,
> A trust from You, our King.
>
> May we Your bounties thus
> As stewards true receive
> And gladly, Lord, as You bless us,
> To You our firstfruits give.

Hearts still are bruised and dead,
   And homes are bare and cold,
And lambs for whom the Shepherd bled
   Are straying from the fold.

To comfort and to bless,
   To find a balm for woe,
To tend those lost in loneliness
   Is angels' work below.

And we believe Your word,
   Though dim our faith, it's true:
What we do for Your people, Lord,
   We do it all for You. Amen.

Esther

Chosen to Save

Theme

The story of Esther is like a modern-day soap opera. God's people had received God's judgment by being sent into captivity because they had turned from Him and His desires for their lives. God provided a rescuer for His people in the person and by the work of Esther. He placed her in a position to serve, using Mordecai in the process. God uses the most unlikely people, including you and me, to share His love and to fulfill His purpose.

Objectives

That by the power of the Holy Spirit working through God's Word, we will

1. demonstrate a willingness for God to use us—our time, talents, and treasures to serve Him and others;
2. demonstrate confidence that God has equipped and will continue to equip us for the tasks He has chosen for us to do in His service;
3. Tell others that God knows our needs, answers our prayers, and uses real people to fulfill His purposes.

Opening Worship

Speak together or sing "Simple Praise for God's Gifts," by Carol and Judy Zehnder. (Sung to the tune of "Simple Gifts," sometimes known as "Lord of the Dance.")

Praise the Lord, Praise the Spirit,
Praise the Son, Praise the Love
That has given me Salvation from above.
Lamb of God, Hope of sinners,
Blessed Savior divine,
Simple gifts You give: Water, bread, and wine.

Weak, lost, my soul in disarray:
My God took my darkness and turned it into day.
By His grace I will serve Him,
By His grace I am free.
I can do all things for He strengthens me.

Into the Lesson

1. What are some indicators that our society is preoccupied with beauty?

2. Why do some condemn this preoccupation with beauty?

Whether this preoccupation with beauty is good or bad depends upon the eye of the beholder. One thing that is certain is that a preoccupation with beauty is nothing new. Apparently beauty was valued in ancient Persia as well. In fact Esther, the heroine in our Bible study, was the winner of a beauty contest in ancient Persia.

Into the Past

Esther placed herself in personal jeopardy in order to do God's will. Read the book of Esther in its entirety. Then complete the following activities.

1. Provide a question for each of the following answers. This is best done by asking a who or what question as in the popular game show "Jeopardy."

   a. Also called Ahasuerus, he ruled from India to Cush, the upper Nile. His palace and court were in the citadel of Susa. He liked to celebrate with opulence and ostentation. He entertained all of the people in the citadel of Susa with a seven-day banquet. Read Esther 1:1–4 as a review.

   b. In charge of the harem, this eunuch assigned Esther seven maids and moved her along with her seven maids into the best place in the harem. Read Esther 2:8–9.

   c. Esther's cousin, he was of the tribe of Benjamin. Esther was actually his uncle's daughter; he was like a father to her, raising her like his own child. He evidenced diligence and protectiveness in checking daily on Esther. He told Esther not to reveal her nationality and she obeyed. His claim to fame was that he discovered an assassination plot against King Xerxes. He told Esther and she told the king. Read Esther 2:10–11.

   d. An orphan, the daughter of Abihail, (Esther 2:7 and 2:15), adopted by Mordecai and raised as his own daughter, she became the Queen of Persia.

   e. Her refusal to come before the king when summoned (Esther 1:10–12) resulted in her banishment as queen.

   f. An important and wealthy subject and a proud and boastful man, he was chosen for honor by Xerxes (Esther 5:11–12). Mordecai irritated him by refusing to bow down to him (Esther 3:5–6). As a result, he looked for a way to destroy not only Mordecai but also all of Mordecai's people, the Jews, for such insolence. He ordered a gallows to be built and planned to ask Xerxes to hang Mordecai.

   g. Natives or inhabitants of ancient Media, a country in southwestern Asia corresponding to northwestern Iran.

   h. Observed about the first of March. Annual festival instituted to commemorate the preservation of Jews in Persia from the massacre designed by Haman. Haman cast lots (pur) to determine the best day for the massacre. Instead, this was the day the Jews were authorized by Xerxes to kill their enemies, all 75,000 of them (Ester 9:18–28).

2. A soap opera typically contains a villain, a heroine, a hero, and a conflict. Roleplay the story with the following episodes.

   a. The Beauty Contest (Esther 1–2)

   b. A Villainous Plot (Esther 3–4)

   c. The Heroine's Deed (Esther 5–8)

   d. The Happy Ending (Esther 9–10)

3. Women's Movement Feared in Persia

   a. Reread Esther 1:10–22. What concern is raised in Esther 1:18?

   Is this still a concern today?

   b. How did God use Queen Vashti to further His purposes? What had Xerxes decreed about Queen Vashti?

   Read Esther 1:19. What was Queen Vashti's fate?

   How can and does God use unpleasant circumstances to accomplish His good purposes today?

4. Dinners and Dreams: God uses everyday events and ordinary occasions to further His purposes.

   a. Read Esther 5:4–8. What was Queen Esther's request? How did the dinner serve God's purpose?

b. Read Esther 7:1–3 and 8:3–6. What new requests did Esther make here?

c. God even used insomnia to further His purposes. Read Esther 6:1–3. What was the result of King Xerxes' sleepless night?

5. The Happy Ending
   a. Read Esther 6:3–13. What dramatic turn of events and example of poetic justice is found in this episode?

   b. How does the story of Haman conclude (Esther 7:9–10)?

   c. What happened to the wealth of Haman (Esther 8:7)?

   d. In Esther 8:3, Esther once again pleaded for her people. How did King Xerxes respond? (Read Esther 8:11–17.)

e. What happened to Mordecai (Esther 9:3–10:3)?

6. God's Timing: Esther didn't go to Xerxes' palace with a deliberate plan to save her people. There was no edict to kill the Jews at the time of the beauty contest. God, however, had His plan even though Esther didn't know at the time how God would use her.

   Develop a timeline of the events in the story.

Into the Present

1. Read Esther 2:12–14 and consider the beautification process. We have a number of sayings about beauty. How do the following sayings relate to Esther's situation?

   a. "Beauty is only skin deep."

   b. "Beauty is in the eye of the beholder."

   c. "Handsome is as handsome does."

2. As people who have received forgiveness of sins and eternal life by God's grace through faith in Jesus' sacrificial death on the cross, we have become beautiful, perfect to God. How does and will God use this beauty, which comes only from Him, to serve Him?

3. *Chutzpa* is a Jewish term for what we might call nerve or audacity. God had gifted Esther with beauty and also courage or *chutzpa*. God used all of these gifts for His purposes. Esther also displayed wisdom and tact in inviting Xerxes and Haman to dinner. Which gift of Esther's do you think was the most important—beauty, courage, wisdom, tact, or loyalty? Which gift would you prefer to have yourself? Why?

4. Whom would you consider to be a rescuer in present times? This might be a significant individual in your faith life or simply someone who figured prominently in your life in a time of need. Explore the vast array of people who influence us as Mordecai did Esther: teachers, grandparents who raise grandchildren, sponsors or godparents, aunts, uncles, cousins, neighbors, friends. Give an example of someone who has been there for you "for such a time as this" (Esther 4:14). How might or has God used you as a rescuer or influence for someone "for such a time as this?"

5. Walking away from rather than confronting problems appears to be on the increase in families today: divorce, child support-delinquent parents, single parents stretched to the limit, neglected elderly parents, abandoned babies. How might God use you—to whom He has demonstrated His great love—to confront sin and assist those hurting because of sin's consequences?

Regarding Your Church Family

1. How are the gifts God has given to members of your congregation being used to serve God?

2. What challenges has your church family been tempted to walk away from?

3. What has God provided to strengthen the faith of the members of your church family so they are motivated and equipped to meet all challenges? (See 2 Timothy 3:14–17.)

Into the Future

1. Esther fasted and asked all the Jews to do the same before she risked her life by appearing unbidden before Xerxes (Esther 4:15–16). What routine activities in your life instill a calmness of purpose and sense of perspective in your life?

2. The Feast of Purim is a Jewish festival that celebrates the story of Esther and the rescue of the Jewish people at that time. Look for events to celebrate in your life. Use suggestions from the booklet produced by the LWML entitled "Traditions for the Christian Family." Choose a specific event to celebrate with your family, such as a Baptism anniversary.

Closing Worship

An Old English Prayer:

Give us, Lord, a bit of sun,
A bit of work and a bit of fun.
Give us in all the struggle and sputter
Our daily bread, and a bit of butter;
Give us health, our keep to make,
And a bit to spare for others' sake;
Give us, too, a bit of song
And a tale and a book to help us along.
Give us, Lord, the strength to be
Our goodly best, brave, wise and free,
Our goodly best for ourselves and others,
Till all men learn to live as brothers. Amen.

Mary Magdalene

"I Have Seen the Lord"

Theme

God chose a woman, Mary Magdalene, to be the first person to see the risen Christ and tell others of the event. Just as the darkness of her grief kept Mary from recognizing Jesus until He spoke her name, so anguish over sin in our lives can keep us from "seeing" the personal relationship God offers to us through His Son's death and resurrection. Our Baptism assures us that we are "dead to sin but alive to God in Christ Jesus" (Romans 6:11). The resulting joy in our hearts bursts forth and compels us to share the Good News with others.

Objectives

That by the power of the Holy Spirit working through God's Word, we will

1. recognize Mary Magdalene's need (and our need) for a personal relationship with her Savior, Jesus;
2. rejoice that the resurrection of our Lord means that our sins are forgiven and we now have a personal relationship with God for eternity;
3. strengthen our personal relationship with Christ as we remember our Baptism daily;
4. witness boldly our joy in Christ's resurrection revealed to us through God's Word.

Opening Worship

Pray responsively Psalm 138:1–3.

Leader: I will praise You, O Lord, with all my heart;

Participants: Before the "gods" I will sing Your praise.

Leader: I will bow down toward Your holy temple

Participants: And will praise Your name for Your love and Your faithfulness,

Leader: For You have exalted above all things Your name and Your word.

All: When I called You answered me; You made me bold and stouthearted. Amen

Into the Lesson

Several Marys are mentioned in the New Testament. Test your knowledge about Mary Magdalene as you mark each statement either + True or ○ False.

___ 1. Mary Magdalene is spoken of in only one gospel.

___ 2. She was an eyewitness of Christ's death.

___ 3. Sometime during his ministry, Christ drove three demons from her.

___ 4. Along with other women, Mary Magdalene went to the tomb Easter morning.

___ 5. She had been a prostitute before Jesus healed her.

___ 6. Mary's home town of Magdala is located on the west coast of the Sea of Galilee near Capernaum.

___ 7. Using her own money to help support their ministry, Mary Magdalene traveled with Jesus and the disciples.

___ 8. She once poured expensive perfume on Jesus' feet and wiped it with her hair.

___ 9. Mary Magdalene ran and told the disciples about the empty tomb after she saw Jesus.

___10. When Jesus spoke her name near the tomb, she was wailing loudly.

Into the Past

1. Luke 8:2 says that Jesus drove seven demons out of Mary Magdalene. The dictionary defines a demon as an evil spirit affecting the mind, heart, and will. We know that a demon is also called a devil, which means "deceiver." The Bible mentions demons more than 75 times, most often in the New Testament. Jesus healed people by driving demons out of them. What can we infer from the information in Luke 8:2 about Mary Magdalene before Jesus healed her? After he healed her?

2. Read Luke 8:1–3. From this reference we know that Mary Magdalene was a woman of means. What did she do with her wealth and time while Jesus' ministry took him from village to village?

3. In all four gospels Mary Magdalene was "watching from a distance" as Jesus was crucified (Matthew 27:55–56; Mark 15:40–41; Luke 23:49; and John 19:25). Take a few minutes to jot down from memory details of Christ's suffering and death. Tell why Mary was so devastated by what she saw.

4. Three gospels (Matthew 27:59–61; Mark 15:46–47; Luke 23:55) tell us that Mary Magdalene followed Joseph of Arimathea to the grave site. Having witnessed the horror of Jesus' death and burial, how does her name Mary, which means "bitter," fit this situation?

5. While all four gospels mention Mary Magdalene's part in the wonderful story of Jesus' resurrection, John takes time to highlight her story. First read aloud John 20:10–18. Then describe the feelings Mary must have experienced as the situation unfolded around her.

6. Compelled by her joy, Mary rushed to tell the disciples the Good News. Think of a situation in your life where your emotions were so heightened that the memory is still vivid today. Recall what took place. Does the memory affect your life now? How?

7. "I have seen the Lord!" (John 20:18). Mary's statement of faith jumps at us from the page. If she were sitting in your group today, what would you ask Mary about her walk with Christ following that first glorious Easter?

8. "Blessed are those who have not seen and have yet believed" (John 20:29). Though we were not eyewitnesses of Christ's resurrection, how does He strengthen and comfort us?

   a. John 14:26–27

   b. Psalm 119:105

   c. 1 Peter 3:21

   d. Acts 2:42

Into the Present

Dr. Henry Van Dyke, a Christian theologian of the last century said: "If four witnesses should appear before a judge to give an account of a certain event, and each should tell exactly the same story in the same words, the judge would probably conclude, not that their testimony was exceptionally valuable, but that they had agreed to tell the same story. But if each man had told what he had seen as he had seen it, then the evidence would be credible. And when we read the four gospels, is not that exactly what we find? The four men tell the same story each in his own way." (*What the Bible Is All About*, by Henrietta Mears. © 1966 Regal Books, Ventura, CA 93003. Used by permission.)

1. Consider for a moment that of the four gospel writers, only Matthew and John saw the risen Christ. Mark and Luke heard the story from eyewitnesses. Yet their accounts are considered no less important. Now it is your turn! You know what Christ's death and resurrection has meant for your life. Imagine that your personal witness of God's love for you will be recorded for the edification of future saints. What will you tell them about your walk with the Savior?

2. Just what did Jesus accomplish through His death and resurrection in the following three areas:

   a. *Sin.* Reflect briefly on sins you have confessed and of which you have been pardoned.

   b. *Death.* How do you show in your daily walk what Paul expressed in these words, "Where, O death, is your sting?" (1 Corinthians 15:55).

   c. *The power of the devil (evil).* Consider the following passages. They affirm the truth that through faith in Christ, we need not fear evil.

   Romans 8:37–39

   1 John 4:2–6

   2 Timothy 1:7

3. In order to help us recognize how Christ's death and resurrection applies to our lives, Dr. Martin Luther suggests that we remember our Baptism daily. For Christians that may mean talking over with the Lord the day's happenings, thanking Him for the blessings, and asking forgiveness where we have gone astray. Share with each other ways that you daily "die to sins and live for righteousness" (1 Peter 2:24).

4. Rejoice in what God's Word has to say about your Baptism.
Galatians 3:26–29

Matthew 28:19

Romans 6:3–4

Ephesians 4:4–5

5. So, having been reassured once more of God's great love for us, we're ready to go tell others. Some people, like Mary Magdalene, witness their faith in front of groups easily. Others find sharing on a one-to-one basis their forte. Choose someone in your group and tell how you see that person witnessing in his or her daily walk.

Regarding Your Church Family

We all share the same joy in Christ's death and resurrection, though how we came to know Him as our personal Savior may vary. Recall the recent witness of a pastor, parent, neighbor, teacher, co-worker, friend, or child that edified you. List a specific way you will thank that person. How might you in turn witness your faith in Jesus to that person? Remember, you are a person of means!

Into the Future

1. Review your day with the Lord each evening before you retire. Reflect on Matthew 6:33–34. Give Him your worries and cares, for the day is over. Humbly ask for forgiveness where you have done wrong. Reflect on blessings granted that day. Then sleep like a baby!

2. Wake up with God's name on your lips. Praise Him, entreat Him to be with you, and go about your day joyfully.

3. Pray that God would give you opportunities to witness for Him. Then watch as He uses the talents He gave you to accomplish much in His name!

Closing Worship

Sing together stanza 1 of "Oh, for a Thousand Tongues to Sing."

> Oh, for a thousand tongues to sing
> My great Redeemer's praise,
> The glories of my God and King,
> The triumphs of His grace!

Dorcas

Willing to Serve

Theme

God has promised us eternal life, and sealed His promise with the death and resurrection of Jesus. The Holy Spirit gives us faith to believe that we are forgiven and grants us gifts we can use to serve God as we help others. Because death no longer holds fear for us, we go about our daily lives joyfully using our talents to share God's love with others.

Objectives

That by the power of the Holy Spirit working through God's Word, we will

1. acknowledge the gifts of eternal life God has granted to all who possess saving faith in Jesus;
2. thank God for the acts of love performed on our behalf and on behalf of others by people like Dorcas;
3. pray that the will of God be shown in our lives through the use of gifts He has given to us.

Opening Worship

Pray together responsively.

Leader: Lord, You destroyed the wall of sin that separated us from You.

Participants: For this our hearts sing!

Leader: Show us what gifts You want us to use as we share Your love with others.

Participants: Yes, Lord, allow us to see the gifts Your Holy Spirit has given us.

Leader: Align our will with Yours, so that we may perform acts of service in Your name, as Dorcas did.

Participants: Use us, Lord, to further the work of Your kingdom.

All: We join with all the saints to praise Your name forever. Amen!

Into the Lesson

Below is a "kindness quilt." Reflect on times in your life when others shared God's love in a tangible way at a time you most needed it. Write in each square a few words describing these incidents.

Choose one event from the quilt and explain the positive effect it had on your walk with the Lord.

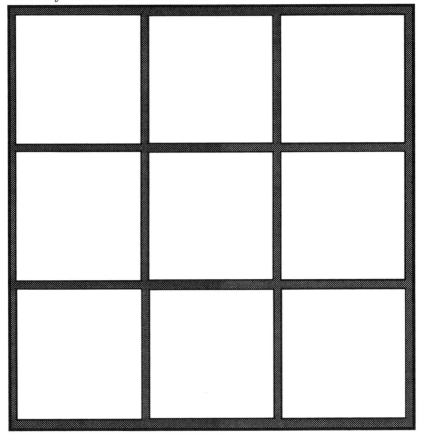

Into the Past

1. Dorcas Societies are common within Christian church bodies. They are known for their charitable deeds. Just who was Dorcas? Read Acts 9:36–43 and identify what she did that inspired so many to follow her example. Acts 9:36 tells us four things about Dorcas.

   a. She was a _____ who lived at Joppa.

   b. Her name is _____ which, when translated, is Dorcas.

   c She was always _____.

   d. She helped _____.

2. Joppa, 38 miles northwest of Jerusalem, served as the main port in Judea. Ruled at various times by Canaanites, Egyptians, the tribe of Dan, Philistines, Assyrians, Persians, and Romans, the fertile Valley of Sharon stretched from Joppa north 30 miles to the headquarters of the Roman occupation, Caesarea. How would Peter's ministry in this area be different than his ministry in Jerusalem? How would it be the same?

3. Since it was one of the few seaports in Israel, Joppa had its share of sailors' families. In those days, families waited months or years to hear from loved ones who had gone to sea. What special needs did they have, especially the wives of the sailors?

4. When Dorcas died, two men were sent to Lydda to urge Peter to come to Joppa (Acts 9:38). Locate these two towns on a map of the Holy Land. Why did they fetch Peter at this time?

5. The widows grieving Dorcas' death showed Peter through their tears the beautiful garments she had made for them (Acts 9:39). Read Acts 9:40–41 and describe Peter's actions.

6. What can we infer from Acts 9:42 about this miracle?

7. The Christians in Joppa saw God's awesome power in action. What passages from Scripture encourage you when you are faced with the death of a loved one?

Into the Present

Edna lived with the specter of death all her life. Born with a deformed lung, she understood as few others could what it is like to gasp for breath. But Edna loved life and embraced it with humble faith. God blessed her with gentleness, good organizational skills, and a beautiful singing voice. She worked, married, raised children, and anticipated grandchildren. When she reached the age of 55, the doctors told her she had from six months to six years to live. So she attached herself to the oxygen tank she called Mariah (her wind) and continued to participate in activities with church, family, and friends,though she no longer had enough breath to sing.

One day during a visit from her two daughters, she experienced a painful physical symptom she didn't recognize. They called the doctor and discovered it was the side effect of some new medication. Their fear subsided, but Edna began to weep. "What's the matter now, Mom, more pain?" asked one of her daughters while the other daughter calmed their father in another room.

"No, it isn't that," said Edna. "It's just that I know my time to go home to the Lord is near. I want to talk about my funeral but your father can't seem to face it."

"Do you know what you want?" her daughter asked as she reached for her mother's hand.

"Yes I do!" Edna said confidently as she wiped away the last bit of tears.

"Let me get a piece of paper and we'll write it down," offered her daughter.

For the next hour they laughed and cried and shared their faith in God's promises as the daughter jotted down her mother's favorite Bible passages and hymns. By the time they finished, a complete order of service had been prepared!

Edna died a year later, after enduring more pain and confinement. The daughter remembered that the paper containing her mother's wishes was tucked into Edna's much-used Bible. The family gathered around as the daughter began to read it. She noticed that Edna had edited her words. Then she stopped and put the paper down, unable to continue. After the very last hymn her mother had written, "Sing joyfully!"

1. "Sing joyfully" was Edna's last witness to her family and it became her epitaph. She knew she would spend eternity with her Lord. What brief statement would epitomize the life of Dorcas? Your life?

2. The New Testament often speaks of eternal life. Write what encourages you from each of the following passages:

   John 3:14–17

   John 5:24

   John 10:27–28

   Romans 6:23

   2 Corinthians 4:16–18

3. Consider what effect your faith in Christ has on others. Look at how you respond to circumstances in your life. Write your own obituary as you would like to be remembered.

4. In John 10:10 Jesus says, "I have come that they may have life, and have it to the full." Share ways that you live life here on earth to the full, knowing that the gift of eternal life is yours.

5. Review the obituary that you wrote. What gifts and talents has God given you? How can you use these to share the warmth of His love with others? Ephesians 4:2–6 supplies the answer. Summarize it in your own words.

Regarding Your Church Family

One way we can bear one another's burdens is through prayer. Write on a slip of paper a burden that weighs heavily on your heart. Exchange papers with a person near you. Pray for each other this week. Include that person's burden in your petitions.

Into the Future

When we are humble before God, He gives us the self-confidence we need to serve others. This week reach out to a person in your community that you notice needs help.

1. Pray for God's guidance in the situation.
2. Give the person a token of your good will such as flowers, a smile, etc.
3. Take time to listen and to acknowledge his or her concerns.
4. Share with him or her how God leads you to solutions to your problems.
5. Remain in touch as the Spirit leads you.

Closing Worship

Speak or sing together "O God of Mercy, God of Light."

O God of mercy, God of light,
    In love and mercy infinite,
Teach us, as ever in Your sight,
    To live our lives in You.

You sent Your Son to die for all
    That our lost world might hear Your call;
Oh, hear us lest we stray and fall!
    We rest our hope in You.

Teach us the lesson Jesus taught:
    To feel for those His blood has bought,
That ev'ry deed and word and thought
    May work a work for You.

For all are kindred, far and wide,
    Since Jesus Christ for all has died;
Grant us the will and grace provide
    To love them all in You.

Interpret What You Have Learned

Below are two Venn diagrams that will help you see the similarities and differences between the six women you have studied. Place the name of each woman outside a different circle. Inside each woman's circle write characteristics and actions that represent her alone. Then look at the section of the circle that intersects with one other woman. Jot down in that space characteristics and actions they both share. Do the same with the rest of the women. Then look for similarities between all three women whose circles intertwine. Place this answer in the center section of each Venn diagram.

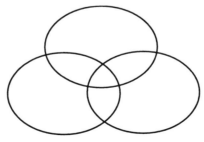

Miriam

First String or Second Fiddle?

Theme

Ask a volunteer to read this section aloud.

Objectives

Ask a volunteer to read these to the group.

Opening Worship

Pray the responsive prayer as indicated. You read the **Leader** sections; the group responds. Or invite a volunteer to read the words of the leader.

Into the Lesson

Direct the class to read the Scripture section silently and respond to the questions. Accept all responses. Bette Midler might best fit Miriam's personality. Miriam might feel comfortable as the star. She was a born leader and enjoyed playing that role.

Group members may take turns reading the paragraphs. The questions are rhetorical; each person may answer for herself. Discuss the concept of a leader also being a servant.

Into the Past

The class may split into smaller discussion groups or remain together as one larger unit to consider these questions.

1. Miriam was independent, trustworthy, quick-thinking, resourceful, a planner for the future, brave, musical, conscious of detail, lively, and connected with God and His Word. A leader needs to be rebellious in the sense that he or she is not blindly bound to convention, but a good leader is committed to the goal and to the group—not focused only on stirring up trouble.

2. She guarded her baby brother, saw to it he was educated by the finest teachers as well as cared for by his own mother, prophesied according to God's direction, and led singing and dancing to celebrate God's deliverance.

3. Judges 4:4—Deborah; 2 Kings 22:14—Huldah; Luke 2:36—Anna; Acts 21:8–9—Philip's daughters.

   These women were called by God to their role. They communicated His Word and will to the people. The Israelites accepted and respected their leadership.

4. Miriam, Aaron, and Moses were siblings. Miriam watched over Moses when he was a baby. She and Aaron seemed to have a close relationship. In most families older children assume a leadership role. Miriam was accustomed to being in charge of her younger brother. Seeing Moses overshadow her in the eyes of God and His people was probably difficult for her to accept. After all, if it hadn't been for her, he would have been killed in infancy.

5. Miriam was jealous of Moses' position. She wanted to be recognized as being as important as he was.

6. Moses' marriage to the Cushite woman was the stated reason for criticism. When people are unhappy or jealous, they grasp at any excuse to complain. Miriam's true agenda was obvious. It is human nature to want credit for our accomplishments and to be envious of others. God, however, calls us to rise above human nature and have the same mindset or attitude as Christ (Phil. 2:5–11). Miriam questioned God's wisdom, setting herself in a position to judge His decisions. In effect, she was making herself into a god, a breach of the First Commandment.

Have group members continue to read aloud the paragraphs that follow.

7. God's reaction was immediate and severe. His anger *burned.* He struck Miriam with leprosy—a symbol of uncleanness, unholiness, and sin.

8. Moses' first reaction was to plead for his sister. His love for her outweighed any competition for God's favor. Moses was an expert at intercessory prayer (Ex. 32:9–14). God listened and responded.

9. Her pride was idolatrous. Her self-centered attitude corrupted her relationship with God. She needed to be reminded of her total dependence on her Deliverer. Her service was meaningful only in the context of a response for the redemption God had provided her.

Read aloud the paragraphs concerning God's deliverance of Miriam from His judgment of leprosy.

10. Give individuals a few moments to complete Miriam's song of deliverance. Ask volunteers to share their versions with the class.

Into the Present

Again, the class may work individually or in groups to complete the questions. Reactions to other people receiving undeserved credit will be strongly negative. "It isn't fair!" is a common response. God doesn't deal with us according to what is "fair," or we would be doomed to punishment. Just as He deals with us according to His undeserved mercy, we, too, can accept others without judgment.

Read Phil. 2:5–11 together as a class. Jesus did not seek His own glory. He willingly took on the role of a servant so He could minister to our needs and glorify His heavenly Father. His ultimate act of service was to die on the cross for our sins. In doing so, He reconciled the world to God. We now have the gift of eternal life if we believe in Him. We are free from the bondage of sin, death, and the power of the devil. His act of service affects everything we are and do.

Allow individuals to rank the activities. Discuss what types of service are difficult and why. Different people have differing interests and gifts. It is ultimately God who makes all service possible. When the recipient of our service is someone we love, we are motivated and empowered beyond reason. It doesn't matter if the people we help are deserving or ungrateful, attractive or repugnant. It is God whom we serve when we serve others.

Continue asking volunteers to read the remaining paragraphs aloud.

Regarding Your Church Family

Read the paragraph and pray the Lord's prayer together, emphasizing the appropriate words. You might hold hands while praying.

Into the Future

Read these suggested activities. Encourage class members to do them throughout the coming days. Ask them to consider sharing results with the class next week.

Closing Worship

Ask the group to express needs and requests and include these in an extemporaneous prayer. Then close by singing or reading the selected stanzas of the hymn.

SESSION 2

Deborah
"I Will Go with You"

Theme

Ask a volunteer to read aloud the theme of the lesson.

Objectives

Invite volunteers to read aloud the objectives.

Opening Worship

Pray the litany together. Then sing or speak stanza 1 of "God of Grace and God of Glory."

Into the Lesson

After participants have completed their individual ways to step out in faith, let volunteers share them. Emphasize that God only requires of us what He has made it possible for us to do.

Into the Past

Have the participants look up the passages in pairs and match the headlines with the verses. The correct answers are (1) 4:16; (2) 4:17–22; (3) 4:1–3; (4) 5:28; (5) 4:3; (6) 4:6a; (7) 4:17; (8) 4:6b; (9) 4:4–5; (10) 4:15; (11) 5:31; (12) 4:7; (13) 4:8; (14) 4:12–13.

Into the Present

Vaya con Dios essentially means "go with God." "God be with you" is another phrase we use to say the same thing. In English, "God be with ye" has been contracted to *good-bye*.

1. Discuss some excuses Deborah might have given for not going along with Barak: I have a job to do here. I have to stay with my husband. It's dangerous out there. I'd rather not. That's a man's job. One woman should not be alone with all those men.
2. Talk about people in the Bible who were told very directly by God to "go" somewhere. Have individuals look up the verses and talk about what the outcome would have been in each case if God had taken no for an answer.

Jonah 1:1–2—God directed Jonah to go to Nineveh and preach against it.

Judg. 6:14–16—God directed Gideon to go and save Israel from Midian.

Ex. 3:10—God directed Moses to go to Pharaoh and bring God's people out of Egypt.

3. Discuss the imperative "*Go* and make disciples of all nations" (Matt. 28:19). Ask, **How do we respond?**
4. Answers will vary.

5. God rescued us from sin and death by sending His only Son Jesus to suffer and die for our sins. Only Jesus' love for us motivates us to step out joyfully in service to Him. When we respond to God's imperative to go with no or not yet we sin. God in His love for us in Christ Jesus continues to offer and to provide repentant sinners full and complete forgiveness for all sin.
6. Have volunteers share one of their gifts and then brainstorm together how such a gift might be used by the Lord.

Regarding Your Church Family

1. Answers will vary. Point out that even what may seem an insignificant task is important to God. To God all service to Him motivated by His love in Christ Jesus is equal, from the seemingly least to the most significant.
2. Answers will vary. Answers may include praying for leaders, speaking positively about the leadership, and trying to place the best construction on leaders' decisions.
3. Answers will vary.
4. Sometimes as we serve God as a supporter of His chosen leadership we may miss out on some of the recognition and glory. Remind participants that we only serve God to give Him the glory. When we seek glory and recognition for our service to Him we are serving Him for the wrong reason. Point out that our sinful self often seeks recognition and glory for service to God. Jesus died on the cross to forgive us of that sin as well as all others.

Into the Future

1. Suggest that participants complete this activity during the week ahead.
2. Discuss how responsibility goes along with being in a position of authority. Christians have a responsibility to make decisions based upon that which God teaches us in Scripture.
3. Deborah's song of victory is an early example of Hebrew poetry. Point out that the song is not rhymed verse but rather a type of ballad recounting the story of the plight of the Israelites and their salvation from their enemies through God's direct intervention.

4. Suggest that participants compose a verse, song, or poem during the next week about a time when God strengthened them beyond their expectation.

Closing Worship

Sing or speak together one or more of the hymns written by women. Pray together the prayer.

Hannah

Return to Sender

Theme

Invite a volunteer to read this paragraph aloud.

Objectives

Ask someone to read aloud the objectives.

Opening Worship

Pray the litany responsively.

Into the Lesson

Have three volunteers read these advice-column letters.

Into the Past

1. Class members may work individually or in small groups to complete the chart.

   Hannah was barren—Elkanah married another wife; grief and sadness for Hannah.

   Elkanah loved Hannah more—Peninnah was jealous; rivalry and grief.

Hannah was distraught—she sulked, prayed, and vowed; bitterness and longing.

Eli sees Hannah—he accuses her of drunkenness; insulted and defensive.

Hannah explains—Eli's blessing; hope, faith, no longer distraught.

Hannah has a child—she praises God and names the child Samuel ("heard of God"); joy.

Hannah keeps her vow—she brings Samuel to Eli to serve; fulfillment and joy.

2. Hannah's despair was transformed by God into joy when she received God's blessing through Eli (1 Sam. 1:15–18).

3. Children were of great importance to Hebrew women because
   Gen. 1:28—it was God's command;
   Deut. 28:4—it was a sign of God's blessing;
   Luke 1:25—it was a social disgrace to be childless;
   2 Kings 4:11–14—economically, women depended on their sons for survival when they became widowed.

4. Hannah wanted to give her husband a son to carry on his name and perpetuate the teachings of God. She was willing to give her son to the Lord.

5. Elkanah's family was probably celebrating the Feast of Ingathering, sometimes called the Feast of Tabernacles, which commemorated God's care in the desert and also celebrated with joy and feasting each year's harvest.

6. It was similar to our Thanksgiving Day. This celebration of fruitfulness and emphasis on family blessings was especially disturbing to barren Hannah.

7. The *Lord Almighty* refers to God as the sovereign power over all beings.

8. Hannah vowed to dedicate her child to the Lord.

9. Hannah voluntarily vowed to give her son to God. This vow would have normally been made by a man as he dedicated His life to God. Rather than bargaining with God she was simply stating a fact. Instead of the conditional "if/then" contract with which we are familiar, the words used in these texts are better translated "when/then." The fulfillment of the condition on God's part is presupposed. Hannah's was a prayer of

faith. She looked ahead to the time God would provide for her need. When that happened, as she knew it would, she would respond by gladly returning this gift to the Giver. Hannah didn't pray with her fingers crossed. She wanted to give the child back. She wanted something valuable to give. This was no rash promise made out of desperation. This was a solid commitment, years in the planning, that was soon to become reality.

10. The word *remembered* means He called the issue to His immediate attention with the intent of acting. It was time—His time—to bring about that which He had intended all along.

11. Discuss together possible blessings derived from Hannah's years of waiting. She developed patience. Her dependence on God grew because she had nowhere else to turn. She developed empathy for others who were discouraged. She learned to be strong in the face of Peninnah's ridicule. She probably appreciated Samuel more because she had to wait so long.

12. Compared with Mary's Magnificat, both songs celebrate God's gift of a child. Both are joyful expressions of praise. Both women rejoice in the Lord and humble themselves. Both give all crdit to God. While Hannah's song foretells a future Messiah, Mary's song exults in that Messiah's birth—God's covenant fulfilled.

Into the Present

1. Allow time for class members to discuss possible replies to the "Dear Sadie" letters.

2. Answers will vary. Sometimes God responds to our prayers by saying yes. At other times in His love for us He might respond not yet or no! God knows what is best for us. Whether God responds yes, later, or no, He continues to love and cherish us.

3. Hannah's peace came from knowing that God had not forgotten her and that she was a child of His blessing. She was praising the giver—God.

4. God's ultimate gift to us is the forgiveness of sins and eternal life He has provided to us through His only Son's death and resurrection. Read aloud the closing paragraph.

Regarding Your Church Family

Encourage the class to pray regularly for others.

Into the Future

It is important to encourage children from an early age to consider such a profession. A simple word of support can motivate a lifetime of commitment.

Closing Worship

Pray each other's petitions. Then sing the hymn.

Esther

Chosen to Save

Theme

Ask a volunteer to read aloud the theme of the lesson.

Objectives

Invite volunteers to read aloud the objectives.

Opening Worship

Sing or speak the opening prayer together.

Into the Lesson

Discuss the questions. Answers will vary. Ask a volunteer to read aloud the paragraph. Discuss what the contest to find a new queen must have been like.

Into the Past

Read aloud the book of Esther. Use the activities in the Study Guide to review.

1. Have the participants read each statement and then ask a who or what question that identifies the person or thing described in the statement (like the TV game show "Jeopardy"). The Scripture references give an additional hint.

The following questions identify the person or thing described in the statements.

   a. Who is **Xerxes**?

   b. Who is **Hegai**?

   c. Who is **Mordecai**? (Note: His role was to be a facilitator like John the Baptist or Aaron or Miriam.)

   d. Who is **Esther**?

   e. Who is **Vashti**? (We don't know the reason that Vashti refused to obey the king. We are told, however, that the king had been partying for many days and may have been inebriated. She was asked to come to this all-male gathering in order to parade her beauty in front of the revelers. We don't know if her refusal was justified. We *do* know that it triggered the chain of events that was to follow in the story of Esther.)

   f. Who is **Haman**?

   g. Who are the **Medes**?

   h. What is the **Feast of Purim**? (Pronounced Poor'-um.)

2. After participants have mastered the facts of the story, have them roleplay the various episodes. Props might include the following hats: a yarmulke (Jewish man's skullcap) for Mordecai, crown for Xerxes, tiara for Esther, a three-cornered hat for Haman.

3. (a) Xerxes' advisors were concerned that Vashti's disrespect for her husband's order would spread to the wives of the nobles who would no longer respect their husbands' authority. (b)Vashti was banished from the king's presence and deposed as queen. Point out that God used the episode between Xerxes and Vashti so that Esther could become queen and so one day He could use her to rescue His people from Haman's evil plot.

4. (a) Esther's first request of King Xerxes was a simple invitation to dinner along with Haman. God used the dinner to expose the treacherous plot of Haman. (b) The second invita-

tion to dinner set the stage for the real request: justice for the evil Haman and salvation for her people, the Jews in Persia. (c) Xerxes couldn't sleep so he got up and read the chronicle of how Mordecai had saved his life.

5. (a) Poetic justice is seen in the complete reversal of situations. Mordecai was honored and richly rewarded while Haman acted as his servant. (b) Discuss the irony of the ending of the story. Haman was hanged on the gallows he had prepared for Mordecai. (c) Xerxes gave Esther Haman's wealth, and Mordecai served as second-in-charge to the king. (d) Instead of being slaughtered as Haman had planned, the Jews are given the right to assemble and protect themselves and to kill those that attack them. (e) Esther 9:3–10:3 documents the rising power of Mordecai.

6. God planted Esther in the king's household so that she could speak on behalf of her people and save them. The events did not transpire in a short period of time but rather took place over many years. The banishment of Vashti took place in the third year of Xerxes' reign (Esther 1:3). Esther came before Xerxes as a queen candidate in the seventh year of his reign (Esther 2:16). The order to kill all the Jews was given in Xerxes' twelfth year of reign (Esther 3:7).

Into the Present

1. (a) Hegai had a prominent role in the beautification of Esther, a one year process! This process took six months of myrrh treatments and six more months of perfumes, cosmetics, and special food. During this time, Esther spent one year among the concubines. As a result, she was savvy and knew palace politics well. Esther was not only beautiful, she was winsome. People liked her. Esther 2:15 indicates that she "won the favor of everyone who saw her." (b) God opened Xerxes' eyes to Esther's beauty and placed her in a position of favor so she could save her people. (c) Esther was not only beautiful, but she had a winsome personality. She also was obedient. She listened to Hegai's suggestions (Esther 2:15) and obeyed Mordecai (Esther 2:22).

2. Emphasize that we who were sinners, ugly to God, were made perfect and beautiful through the blood of Jesus shed on the cross. Answers will vary.

3. Esther had the courage to honor and respect the ties of blood and affection, even when these detracted from her prestige and placed her in a dangerous position. When she stepped forward and acknowledged her Jewish heritage, she risked her position as queen and her very life. Answers will vary. Discuss the fact that all these attributes are gifts from God.

4. Answers will vary. Urge participants to share significant people in their lives who offered their advice, counsel, and encouragement during difficult times. Remind participants that only God's love in Christ motivates us to encourage others as they struggle during difficult times. Other motivations for helping those in need are usually self-serving.

5. Discuss how God equips or prepares us for what He wants us to do. Through faith strengthened by the Holy Spirit working through Word and sacrament God enables and empowers us to confront *lovingly* problems that may arise in our church, community, family, society, etc. As we share God's Law (what God desires of us) and God's Gospel (what God has done for us in Christ Jesus) with others the Holy Spirit works to touch their lives with healing, encouragement, comfort, and peace.

Regarding Your Church Family

Ask a volunteer to read aloud the questions. Answers will vary.

1. Answers will vary.

2. Answers will vary. Examples might include the changing ethnic makeup of your neighborhood, demands for alternate worship styles and music, declining membership, etc. God uses His people to serve those in need.

3. God has provided Scripture through which the Holy Spirit works to strengthen the faith of believers so they are "thoroughly equipped for every good work."

Into the Future

1. Prayer and fasting were a part of Esther's risk-taking. She also asked others to pray for her. Suggest that since God tells us the Holy Spirit works through God's Word to strengthen faith, Bible reading and Bible study are important routine activities.

2. Suggest that participants consider this activity.

Closing Worship

Speak the closing prayer together.

Mary Magdalene

"I Have Seen the Lord"

Theme

Invite a volunteer to read aloud the theme of the lesson.

Objectives

Invite volunteers to read aloud the objectives.

Opening Worship

Read responsively Ps. 138:1–3.

Into the Lesson

Ask participants to complete the true/false exercise silently. If the group is comfortable doing so, poll results before discussing answers.

1. **False**—All four gospels mention Mary Magdalene (Matt. 28:1; Mark 16:1; Luke 8:2; Luke 24:10; John 20:10–18).
2. **True**—All four gospels verify this.

73

3. **False**—Seven demons were cast out of Mary Magdalene (Luke 8:2).
4. **True**—See the references in number 1.
5. **False**—Though popular movies, church tradition, and legends promote this as fact, Scripture does not. The confusion usually stems from Luke 7:36–50, where Jesus forgives a sinful woman, and John 8:3–11, where Jesus forgives a woman caught in adultery. Since there is no mention of either woman's name, there is no reason to believe that it is Mary Magdalene.
6. **True**—It is just three miles from Capernaum.
7. **True**—Note Luke 8:1–3.
8. **False**—This is a reference to the sinful woman in Luke 7:36–50.
9. **False**—See John 20:1–18. She raced back to tell the disciples about the empty tomb, returned with Peter and John, stayed after they left, then saw Jesus.
10. **True**—Movies may portray her sobbing demurely, but Jesus asked, "Why are you wailing?"

Into the Past

1. Since God's Spirit cannot co-exist with evil, her life was marked by separation from God. Once Jesus drove out the demons, she was able to experience His love. She understood as few others could the terror of evil, and so her gratefulness overflowed in her devotion to Jesus and His ministry. Mary served and supported Jesus with her time, talents, and treasures.
2. Luke 8:1–3 says she traveled with Jesus and the disciples. Discuss ways in which Mary Magdalene and the other women supported them.
3. You may wish to list events surrounding Jesus' passion on a chalkboard or a large sheet of newsprint.
4. Answers will vary. It was a bitter experience to watch the person who saved her life treated with such utter contempt. Without Jesus to live for, life lost its meaning and became bitter.
5. Showing both His humanity and deity, Jesus comforted Mary and then told her not to touch Him. Soon Mary would understand that the Holy Spirit would supply her needs (John 16:5–16). Mary's emotions moved from the depths of despair

to elation within a few moments. Allow time for participants to choose words that help them see the awesome revelation Mary received.

6. Participants may mention events in their life that involve positive or negative emotions (e.g., a wedding, funeral, disaster, rejection, birth, etc.). Emphasize that feelings are not good or bad. It is our response to them that determines what effect they will have on our lives and the lives of others.

7. Encourage imaginative responses.

8. The Holy Spirit guides us today. God's Word, Holy Baptism, and the Lord's Supper are the means of grace through which the Holy Spirit works to strengthen and comfort us. (a) John 14:26–27—The Holy Spirit comforts and guides us and gives us His holy peace; (b) Ps. 119:105—His Word is a light for our path as we walk through life; (c) 1 Peter 3:21—Baptism has removed the stain of sin; (d) Acts 2:42—We are strengthened through the teaching of His Word, fellowship, the breaking of bread, and prayer.

Into the Present

Some participants may wonder about variations in the gospel accounts. Dr. Van Dyke's illustration helps us see that when we put the four books together, a more complete picture unfolds.

1. Take a moment to pray about what the Lord might want each person to learn as he or she answers this question. Participants may want to spend more time on this question than today's Bible study permits. If so, plans may be made to share responses during the next session.

2. Dr. Martin Luther said that Christ conquered sin, death, and the power of the devil. This summarizes what Christ accomplished through His death and resurrection. (a) No one need share this aloud. We do not want to dwell on past mistakes that are forgiven. The purpose of looking "briefly" at our sins is to recognize that God through Christ has fulfilled the Law for us (Col. 2:13–15). (b) Personal reflection would be appropriate here. (c) How comforting it is to know that our loving God protects us from the evil in this world (2 Thess. 3:3).

Rom. 8:37–39—Nothing, not even demons, can separate us from the love of God in Christ Jesus our Lord.

1 John 4:2–6—The one who is in us is greater than the one who is in the world.

2 Tim. 1:7—God gave us a spirit of power, love, and self-discipline.

3. By sharing ways they incorporate meditation on God's Word (listening to God) and prayer (talking to God) into their daily walk, participants encourage and inspire each other.

4. **Gal. 3:26–29**—All who are baptized have been clothed by God with Christ Jesus and are one in Christ.

   Matt. 28:19—We baptize in the name of the Father, Son, and Holy Spirit.

   Rom. 6:3–4—Through Baptism we were buried with Jesus into death and raised from the dead through the glory of the Father to live a new life.

   Eph. 4:4–5—There is one faith, one Lord, one Baptism …

5. You may wish to be the first person to acknowledge another's witness so that others will share more readily.

Regarding Your Church Family

Ask participants to read the paragraph silently and circle one of the witnesses listed. Begin a prayer of thankfulness to God for putting that person in your life. Allow participants to add to the prayer by naming their special witnesses. Conclude the prayer by asking God to help you boldly declare the wonders He has performed as you witness your faith in Jesus to that person and others.

Into the Future

Urge participants to follow the suggested activities during the week and into the future.

Closing Worship

Sing or pray together stanza 1 of "Oh, for a Thousand Tongues to Sing."

Dorcas

Willing to Serve

Theme

Read the theme aloud together.

Objectives

Invite volunteers to read aloud the objectives.

Opening Worship

Pray the responsive prayer.

Into the Lesson

Tell participants they may write a different instance in each square. The acts of love may vary from a smile or a hug to the pastor's sermon the day they were married, or the many hours a parent sacrificed to help them. Encourage them to finish and add on to the "quilt" in their private devotions throughout the week.

Into the Past

1. Traditionally, Dorcas Societies have been sewing circles. Brainstorm ways participants see church sewing circles doing acts of service in churches today. How have they branched out into other areas besides sewing? Coupon clipping? Visits to the sick? etc.

   Ask volunteers to read the account of Dorcas in Acts 9:36–43. Remind them that according to Acts 9:31, the church enjoyed peaceful growth at this time.

. (a) Dorcas was a disciple who lived at Joppa. (b) Her name is Tabitha or Dorcas. *Dorcas* is the Greek version of the Hebrew name *Tabitha*, which means "gazelle" or "fawn". (c) She was always doing good. (d) She helped the poor.

2. Peter would discover and accept different traditions. For instance, Hebrews in this area might prepare a body for burial and wait three days to bury the person. In Jerusalem, a body was placed in the ground within 24 hours after death. Food here often came from the sea. Peter would soon be told by the Lord that it is acceptable to eat things previously forbidden. His message of Christ's redemption remained the same wherever he went.

3. During long separations, families of seafaring men coped with uncertainty about their return. Women made all the decisions regarding family life while the men were away, then had to step back and assume different roles when their husbands came home. There was no way to contact the men if family crises arose. These women relied on the kindness of others in such situations.

4. Lydda is located about twelve miles southeast of Joppa on the way to Jerusalem. The Christians at Joppa may have sent for Peter to comfort them, help in the burial, or they may have hoped for a miracle.

5. Peter sent the grieving widows out of the room, knelt, prayed, and said, "Tabitha, get up."

6. Because the passage says people believed in the Lord as a result of this miracle, we know that Peter gave all the credit to God.

7. Give participants time to share Bible references.

Into the Present

Edna's life might spark responses to these questions: How did Edna's physical problems actually help strengthen her character? What might have caused her husband's difficulty in accepting her imminent death?

1. An epitaph requires a brief summation of one's life into one phrase or sentence. Think of words you have seen on tombstones. Edna knew that she would be singing in heaven for eternity. Dorcas' epitaph might use the words *sewing* or *caring*. Answers will vary.

2. **John 3:14–17**—The Old Testament prophecy of a Savior is fulfilled by Christ, who came to save, not condemn. Those who believe have eternal life.

   John 5:24—Through faith in God and the saving work of Jesus we cross over from death to life.

   John 10:27–28—Jesus knows and protects all who follow Him. No one and no thing, including physical death, can take us away from Him!

   Rom. 6:23—Eternal life is a gift from God through Christ.

   2 Cor. 4:16–18—Though we see our physical world decaying as time passes, our spiritual renewal each day reminds us that we will live eternally. We live by faith, not by sight.

3. An obituary is a notice of a person's death that includes a short biographical account of a person's life. Have a few examples from newspapers on hand. Since this exercise is introspective and highly personal, participants may wish to finish their obituary during private devotions later in the week. Emphasize this activity as one more way to witness faith in Christ.

4. While we are still here on earth, Christ tells us that following Him allows us to live life "to the full." God's love for us overflows so that we share His love with others.

5. Eph. 4:2–6 tells us that humility before God gives us confidence before people. God's love for all people guides our actions toward others.

Regarding Your Church Family

Have slips of paper ready to distribute to participants.

Into the Future

The participants may choose a neighbor, relative, churchmember, or stranger. Gather in a circle, holding hands as you pray for God's guidance in this outreach. Each person may add his or her praise and petitions, then gently squeeze the hand of the next person to signal his or her turn.

Closing Worship

Sing or pray together the hymn "O God of Mercy, God of Light."

Interpret What You Have Learned

The six women studied are Miriam (Ex. 15:19–21), Deborah (Judges 4–5), Hannah (1 Sam. 1:1–2:11), Esther (Esther), Mary Magdalene (John 20:10–18), and Dorcas (Acts 9:36–43). This activity may be accomplished more quickly and comprehensively using small groups that brainstorm answers for several minutes. Then draw large Venn diagrams on a chalkboard or large sheet of newsprint. Record each group's responses on these diagrams, encouraging participants to give reasons for their answers. More than two Venn diagrams may be needed, as names may be grouped in different ways.